All My Love,

Aubrey

All My Love,

Aubrey

Aubrey Jane Jones

Illustrations by Becki Beasley (pg. 8 & 128), Ryan Honaman (pg. 54), Laura Lilley (pg. 80) & Amy Grace Stephen (pg. 106)

Cover art by Becki Beasley
Cover design by Aubrey Jane Jones

ISBN 978-93-5891-198-5

For Beckett and Huxley

May you live ever confidently in your truth

To all the eggs,

Cracked and uncracked

May you find hope in these words.

May you see through the nouns and the verbs.

May you live your truth in confidence.

I see you; I promise.

All My Love,

Aubrey

Contents

Backward 9

Forward 55

Inward 81

Outward 107

backward

Firsts 15

Behind Locked Doors 18

Three Words that Change Everything:

A Story Unfinished 22

Renovations 24

Time 28

My List of Names 32

Letting Go 35

Letters to a Younger Me 37

A Conditional Affection 48

What I Got 51

All My Love, Aubrey

Introduction: *Backward*

Dear Reader,

I thought it only fitting to tell you a little about myself before I start baring my soul to you. In my 34 short years, I've lived a lot of life. I've gone through more heartbreak and healing than I ever thought possible. I've seen moments so dark, I thought there would be no way out. I've experienced bliss so profound that if my life were to have ended, I know I'd have lived a full one. What you are about to read is the result of that journey. The highs and lows of being a transwoman in 2023, of living 33 years in a body that wasn't mine.

The first momentous shift in my life happened after I left organized religion in 2020. After eleven years of working fulltime as a youth pastor for several churches in Washington DC and Pennsylvania, I knew that the only way I would ever find growth would be to leave it all behind me. I was thirty-two years old, in the best shape of my life, and loving the freedom that I finally found in releasing all the expectations and limitations that ministry work placed on me and my family. Soon after, I started my own spiritual coaching practice and began seeing clients who were either leaving the church or seeking a greater understanding of their spiritual selves.

In an effort to broaden my reach and find new clients, I became heavily involved in the *#exvangelical* world of Instagram, often posting stories of the extent to which the church had affected my spiritual development over the years and the hold that it still had over me. Throughout that first year, I made a bunch of new connections and some great friends that I've grown to love dearly. I really enjoyed how much internal processing I was able to do in writing those few short paragraphs of description after a post and the connection that so many amazing people had with my words.

In response to this course, a chorus of voices were saying that white, cisgender men, like Harris, needed to step out of the spotlight and open space for minority voices. As someone who identified as a white, cisgender male at the time, I felt an incredible pressure to do just that. The pressure wasn't from other people, it came from somewhere within me, but there was something else stirring. It made me start to question who I was, because something about what was going on just didn't sit right. I dove deeper into myself to figure out what was going on.

When I was a child, I secretly wished I was born a girl. I would perform little 'spells' in hopes I would wake up one day in a different body, with the life I'd always wanted. It wasn't until I was twelve or thirteen years old that I discovered I wasn't the only one that felt that way. I was home sick from school one day watching TV when a documentary came on talking about people that underwent "sex changes." The early afternoon documentary that ran on Lifetime followed several transgender women for the few months that led up to their gender confirmation surgeries, and as they shared their stories, I remember feeling awe struck. For one, that surgeries like that existed, and two, that I was not the only one that had known my whole life that I was living in a body that wasn't mine. For the first time in my life, I felt seen. For the first time in my life, I knew I wasn't alone.

This was the same time of my life that I was getting more involved with the church. I grew up in a moderate United Methodist church with a very conservative, evangelical youth ministry. Having never been a popular person in school, youth group became the place where I felt loved and accepted. I dove in, headfirst. I did my very best to walk the line they set out for me. The line that promised I would find peace, love, and healing.

Two decades later, I finally found my freedom, and not even a year after that, my transgender egg cracked and all these suppressed memories from my childhood came flooding back. I came out to my partner as transgender in October of 2021 and started Hormone Replacement Therapy the following month. Soon after, in December, I came out as a transwoman to all my friends and family.

These poems are about that journey. The journey I took through 3 decades of living my life in a body that never felt right. The journey I started after I found my freedom, and all the joys, trials, and fallout that came with it.

I poured all of myself out onto these pages. I hope they move you. I hope they help humanize the trans community. I hope you feel seen and know, maybe for the first time in your life, that youre not alone.

All My Love,

Aubrey

Firsts

The first time I looked in the mirror
and saw her instead of him,
was a moment that took my breath away.
My long empty cup was filled to the brim.

The first time I heard my kids call me mom,
my eyes filled with tears.
Like a long-forgotten tune remembered.
Their soft voices were music to my ears.

The first time I spoke my name out loud,
I knew my life had changed.
A transformation was taking place,
as chaos rearranged.

The first time a stranger called me ma'am,
my heart certainly skipped a beat.
It took more than a moment to fully realize
they were even talking to me.

The first time my mom called me her daughter
was the moment that I knew,
though my new life was hard to accept,
her love for me was true.

The first time I ever kissed a boy
felt like fireworks began.
Radiating outward and tingling my body
from somewhere deep within.

The first time I was offered unwanted affection
from a man I didn't know
My body tensed in fight or flight
then suddenly I froze.

The first time I felt that terror fill me,
familiar to many others,
I found a new appreciation for all the powerful women,
all the sisters and the mothers.

The first time I found a tribe of women,

a place I knew where I belonged,

I finally understood the sisterhood,

for which I'd always longed.

I never thought, at thirty-three,

there'd still be so many firsts.

I never thought, even after I changed,

there'd still be so much hurt.

Life is full of ups and downs,

of joy, of pain, of sorrow,

but there's nothing I wouldn't give to live

my truth again tomorrow.

Behind Locked Doors

An open door, soul laid bare
Authentic bliss with curly hair
Desire for witness in my uniqueness
Soon to be hidden by misguided politeness

A hope for acceptance, for full completeness
But a welling understanding of my profound difference
I could never fit in to their standard mold
None to reflect what I knew in my soul

Coldness, rejection, letting go of my inner truth
A child's satisfaction was coming loose
So, I helped her find a place to hide
Out of the light, in darkness, in lies

Lies buried her deep, behind a door tightly locked
Out of fear that my truth would be shamed and be mocked
So, I hid her away, ignoring her cries
Drowning her out, but I didn't realize

The shame I'd been feeling, wasn't from culture

It sprouted and fed on my refusal to love her

I couldn't accept her, started believing the lie

She'd never be a part of me, I was letting her die.

Dormant and lost, behind a door long forgotten

In a part of my soul I thought useless and rotten

It was there that she waited, lovingly patient

Waiting for me to come and unlock it.

Discarded completely, through sheer force of will

Left a hole in my heart that I needed to fill

Religion, morality, and disassociation

But no god could cure the sadness I lived in

Deeper and deeper, I searched for the answer

My growing despair became an all-consuming cancer

When my hope was all lost, or so that it seemed

She revealed herself again, as if hidden in dreams.

Behind all the boxes I'd thought of as trash

Was a door long forgotten, one I almost walked past

A door that'd been sealed, knob tarnished with rust

A sign saying, "Danger, please keep this door shut"

I cleared the debris and made my way forward

The air stood silent, save for a creak in a floorboard

Before the door I stood, but it needed a key

One I thought lost to my dark history

Hopelessly resolved, the door couldn't be opened

I shoved my hands in my pockets and found something forgotten

Slowly, as tears welled up in my eyes,

I unlocked the door to see what was inside.

Smiling, she stood there, arms opened and wide

She was waiting for me, knowing I tried

My eyes meeting hers, I felt the love and the care

And that hole in my heart was no longer there

With joy and with love, I welcomed it all

Claiming the part, I had thought was a flaw

What alchemized despair into hope? I would posset

Was the moment we both stepped out of the closet.

Three Words that Change Everything:
A Story Unfinished

"I love you," they said, on bated breath
anxiously awaiting whatever came next
Her head lay back, eyes stared at the ceiling
Mind racing and searching for what she was feeling
She felt a connection, but love is complex

She'd said it before, in relationships past.
She'd said it to people who never said it back.
She knew in the silence, seconds became minutes
She knew that their heart was racing to its limits
Would this time be for real? True love at last?

But loves from her past still swirled in her head
She knew what was expected, what she could have said.
Love lost left her broken, building walls ever higher,
But the one lying next to her had kindled a fire.
Having been there before, she feared where it led.

A connection had become a crush, and a crush became feelings.
Could this lead to her heart's much-needed healing?
With only one way to know, one way to find out,
The words, "I love you, too," came out of her mouth.
Her walls set free what they'd been concealing.

Fast-forward a decade, thru marriage and kids,
That love was foundation of all that they did.
But ceaselessly time caused their feelings to change.
The love was still there, but something else rearranged.
And she sent her heart back behind the walls it once hid.

Her story's not over, as time will yet tell,
As she longs to heal her fiercely broken shell.
She's praying for patience, love to find her once more,
But right now, she's still lying in tears on the floor.
As she learns to love herself, her despair will dispel.

Renovations

My heart holds a room that was a favorite of mine.

Its walls painted thick with love and with time.

Covered with photos of memories long past,

shared with someone I loved; a love meant to last.

We made her a place to live in my heart.

She was invited to stay, right from the start.

The time it began holds moments I'll cherish.

It started with dinner and continued with marriage.

Our friends and our families felt the joy and the care,

in this room we created, in this time we both shared.

But I struggle to consider what has now since become,

of this room we created, now that its purpose is done.

What wish do I have? That she'd chosen to stay,

holding true to our long-ago promises made.

"To have and to hold, till death do us part."

Made out of love that was kindled from spark.

But the frames got obscured with long ignored dust.

Our memories, our connection, had tarnished to rust.

The room in my heart was burning to ash,

and it wasn't long after that I heard it all crash.

A part of my soul had been severed and lost.

A part of my identity had been crumpled and tossed.

My room left destroyed, in chaos, a mess.

My heart had been mated in this life game of chess.

Now left with the ruins of what had once been,

I feel too ashamed to let anyone in.

I won't be fooled again, sow my heart for your reaping.

But as I thicken my walls, I hear someone weeping.

Hidden inside this sad lonely room

is a sad lonely girl in the debris that'd been strewn.

Not long ago, she'd made herself seen,

all full of hope, and joy, and unrealized dreams.

But instead of being met with joy and elation,
she'd been the cause of all the destruction.
I wanted to blame her for causing all this,
for all the lost memories and future I'd miss.

I wanted to yell, to scream, and to cry.
I wanted her dead. I wanted to die.

But meekly she spoke, "Please, I'll help you rebuild,"
"Please don't destroy it, it could be refilled."

Her voice was familiar, both gentle and kind.
I knew her from somewhere, or from some other time.
Then it struck me, deep down, like the roots of a tree.
This girl deserves everything because this girl is me.

So, I knelt down beside her and looked into her eyes.
Then holding her close, we started to cry.
The pain we'd experienced needed to heal,
and it started to lessen, so we struck up a deal

We're still cleaning up this mess that I made.

There's a long way to go, but the sadness will fade.

Together we're creating a home for us both.

A place of love and of joy, of connection and growth.

Time

It hurts.
It hurts so profoundly.

A pain in the depths of my soul
that can't be ignored.

Time is an evil bitch.

She gives you a moment,
but won't let you hold her

Sometimes the moment feels like a lifetime.
Sometimes a lifetime feels but a moment

The more I cling
the more she slips,
slips through the fabric of my being
to the soul that longs for her.
That longs for love.
That longs for her match in another

I thought I found that match.

I thought I found it many times before,

But every time,

every time she rips it away.

She rips away all of it

to be lost

lost to history.

Time offered me a love more meaningful

than a billion others

But she stripped that away too.

I lost the one my soul felt safe with.

that my soul felt alive with

felt completely free with

I fight with her

fight with time

I yearn for that love we had.

I know I'll never stop,

never stop loving them.

No matter how much I convince myself I have.
No matter how many lifetimes I live.

So, I lie and wait.
I wait for the thing I long for most
The one I treasure more deeply
Then the time I exist in.

But I'm waiting for someone
whom time has already stolen
and memories keep raw

These wounds will never heal.

She is robbing me of my joy
of my passion,
of my pleasure.

All time left me with is pain.
All she left me with is heartbreak.
She's convinced me tomorrow won't be better
that all tomorrow brings is more sorrow.

I wish she'd bring me peace,

bring me joy again.

Maybe she will,

but maybe that's another lie.

The lie she tells.

told to deceive me

into believing there is light in my future,

That there will be joy again.

But she hides the lie deep within herself.

Because time will always rob me of the people I love.

Nothing

No one

can escape her grasp.

My List of Names

I feel but a fool.
A fool to fall in love
again, and again, and again

A fool to pretend
It was anything but
love.

The list of names I gathered
grew ever longer.
With each passing stanza,
a discovery:
Not one of them had my name of theirs.

Except for one,

But the name they scribed was an illusion,
a lie.
A mask I gave them,
Completely unaware
of its grasp.

I've since dissolved that name,
given my soul permission to transcend it.
But the one who etched it on their list
did it in stone.

And their mark
was too dark
too deep
for them to erase
and rewrite.

Its depth left a scar
an everlasting reminder
of a lie.

The unconscious lie
the one I told
the one I believed
I believed because the alternative
was a burden
a burden I didn't have the strength to carry.

It was my truth

My truth that I didn't have the strength to nurture

to grow

to live

to love

to love enough to see on my list

the name that had always been first

my name,

Aubrey.

Letting Go

My heart left broken

With chest ripped open

A sorrow, a loss, just empty emotion.

Future hopes, my plans

Now gone, vacant hands

Like a traveler lost in foreign lands.

No guide, no compass

Nor peace to be found

A dance without rhythm on unsolid ground.

Afraid, I go forth

To a land yet known

My heart filled with dread of being alone.

But please, this next era,

One I choose to mold,

Bring fresh chances, new things to behold.

So, each step I take

Each memory I make

I unfold myself to wholly create.

All My Love, Aubrey

Letters to a Younger Me

I.

Dear seven-year-old me,

You're not broken,
You're not a burden,
you never were.

It's not weird that most of your friends are girls,
or how much you love your hair and your curls.
It's not your fault the boys make you cringe,
and you always find yourself out on the fringe.

I'm sorry you were bullied for the clothes that you wore,
For your shorts being too short
For liking music more than sports,

I know you try hard to make it make sense,
analyzing everyone to find where you fit in,
wishing you'd been born as anyone else,
wishing that magic could heal how you felt.

I wish I could hug you and comfort your pain.
I wish I could tell you and somehow explain.
You are never alone. I am right by your side,
and one day you'd wake up without needing to lie.

That magic you hope for is REAL, and here's proof,
in twenty-six years, you'll be living your truth.
Till then, please be patient and know that you're safe,
and one day, very soon, you WILL find your place.

All My Love,
Aubrey

II.

Dear thirteen-year-old me,

I know how much puberty sucks.

I know how much you hoped you'd be fixed,
hoped this change would stop your mind playing tricks.

I know that it hurt when you lost your best friend,
simply because of the body you live in.
You'll be friends again, of that there's no doubt,
but you're both in a closet you first need to come out.

You live in an era when difference is shamed.
But the world's growing up and one-day things will change.
I love you for all your bravery and strength,
your willingness to take risks and make positive change.

I wish I could say life would be easy from here,
but something is coming to hold you captive for years.
There's a devil that's lurking with a mouth full of lies,
and he'll promise to fix what's held broken inside.

He'll say you're not broken, just in need of a savior,

who takes the form of a babe who was laid in a manger.

He'll say he'll transform you, make you perfect and new,

by taking away all that makes you truly you.

I'm saddened to think that he'll steal your heart,

by claiming he'll make you a pure work of art.

And you'll try and you'll try to make it all work,

forced to bury me deeper, with all your pain and your hurt.

"God has a plan for you," and believing that's true,

You'll deny and forget what makes you truly you.

But I'll be here

through it all,

I know you struggle to see.

But one day you'll become

who you were truly meant to be.

All My Love,

Aubrey

III.

Dear twenty-two-year-old me,

Congratulations!

You made it through all the heartbreak and stress.
College is over and you did your best.
I know how it seems real life has begun,
That the world stands before you and there's work to be done.

You'll make friends and find love, settle down, and enjoy.
And in no time at all, you'll welcome two boys.
But I know that you know there's a weight you still carry,
a long-forgotten part still lays covered and buried.

One day you'll discover it, your eyes will soon see.
The truth you hid safely will one day be free.
But still, my dear, there's much work to be done,
so much healing and changes are still yet to come.

I know the path forward seems entirely clear,
but I've been where this path ends and the answer's not here.
There's much more to life than the church's expectations.
More peace, more acceptance, more love, more sensation.

I wish if I asked you to leave, you would listen,
so you'd not have to grieve losing all you believed in.
But if not for this path as part of your life,
you'd miss out on your boys, you'd miss out on your wife.

So I'm sorry, for all the inevitable pain.
Trust the process, without hurt, there's no growth, no positive change.
Keep your head high and be rooted in love.
A love that comes from within and not from above.

Keeping "his" commandments won't hold the answers you seek.
They're found in the love you give and company you keep.
Those that love with condition, aren't loving you properly,
and when you leave them behind, you create space
to love more abundantly.

I love you my dear, and I can't wait to meet you.

There are only a few short more years to get through.

All My Love,

Aubrey

IV.

Dear thirty-one-year-old me,

Wow, my dear, it's been one hell of a ride.

You made it out, no need to pretend, no need to hide.

Now to only look deeper and find what's inside.

Trust me, my love, I know it's hard letting go.

Over a decade of work, now with nothing to show.

But the time you've spent growing is worth all the spent energy.

You discovered who you are, and who you know you could be.

I greatly applaud your courage, your tenacity.

It took guts to walk away and explore life's complexity.

But this is just the beginning, your next big step forward,

And I can't wait for you to discover what you're moving toward.

You know now, quite well, some will never understand,

why you did what you did, and I'm not sure they can.

There are some who'll surprise you and stick by your side.

Their love's not for what you did, but who you are inside.

So, take every wave, enjoy every sunrise.

Live deep in compassion and love the whole ride.

Take risks and take chances, this is YOUR life to live

Be yourself, without fear. Freely love. Freely give.

Soon, very soon, as you stop living their standard,

and stop conforming your life to the image they planted,

We'll meet, face to face, deep down in your soul,

and you'll finally find out why you never felt whole.

Till then, I'm waiting, for you to discover,

what little is left for you to uncover.

So continue the search, and soon you will find,

that I've been longing to meet you, so you can finally shine.

I promise I'm sending all the love I can gather.

You're so close, nearly there, just a little bit farther.

        All My Love,

        Aubrey

V.

Dear thirty-three-year-old me,

Oh, how I love you, my dear.
This is it. It's our time, our year.

I can't wait to meet you.

I can't wait to hug you.

I can't wait to see your smile
see your eyes light up

When you realize who I am.

When you realize who YOU are.

All My Love, Now and Forever,

Aubrey

A Conditional Affection

All it took was a moment
a moment is all it ever takes.
An empty promise to cease this torment
My future now God's to recreate.

I was their type, the one they wanted
The catch they desired to manipulate.
They lured me in with all that they flaunted
Using "God loves you" to cover their hate

Their hatred of difference, of the one set apart
Deeming me full of sin and flawed
I'd be helpless to correct my evil heart
Unless I answered their god as he called

Like an arid sponge, I absorbed,
desperate to end all my guilt and my pain
No healing was found, I just chose to ignore
the quiet voice inside my brain.

That inner voice so desperate to tell

my truth had value and worth

In searching for peace, I lost myself

In finding heaven, I found a curse.

Willingly broken to uncover my calling

my life wasn't mine to discover

Ignoring my truth, I started falling

bruising my soul with no way to recover

Trying to find meaning, a life that I loved

Seeking the life I'd been promised was there

Finding only excuses amidst all the sludge

Stealing my image from my truth without care

Their love was not free

It came with a price.

There was no love for any

unless it came with a prize

A conditional affection
wrapped up in a bow
An exceptional expectation
to never find growth

I never matched their imagined perfection
nor measured up to the mark they drew
Always praying that I could be the exception
Never getting my chance to live out my truth

So, I left them behind
to find what I knew
to freely love and be kind
to all of creation, not just their few.

What I Got

I felt like I never deserved it
Never worthy of it
of the sacrifice it required
like I had to prove myself worthy
To work for it
Every action
Every single day.

Even when freely given
it never felt free
it never felt like anything.

I needed to earn it
I needed to work for it
And after I got it,
it was just as easy to forfeit
If I didn't keep earning it
proving I deserved it.

If I stopped the work,
I'd lose it forever.

And when I gave my love
to someone else
what I expected in return
was a standard just as unattainable
as the one I forced on myself
as the one forced on me.

Aubrey Jane Jones

forward

What I Wanted.. 61

Tides and Storms...................................... 63

A Brother Lost... 66

Reflection of Dreams.............................. 69

Please Complete Me................................ 71

Thirst & Love... 72

& Dust.. 73

The One.. 74

To All Life's Questions............................ 75

To Love Myself Again.............................. 78

Introduction: *Forward*

Dear Reader,

I took my first dose of HRT on November 15, 2021. I vividly remember standing in my kitchen with my partner, Kendra that evening after getting home from my first endocrinologist appointment with a few small pills in my hand. Kendra, full of love and support, took a picture to mark the start of this next chapter of my story.

I had so much excitement and anxiety going into that appointment. I'd been out of the closet for about a month, told my parents, siblings, and the school that my oldest attended, but would still leave the house dressed in my masculine clothes, held back by fear. As I was getting ready for my appointment that day, I made the choice to push past that fear and fully embrace my truth. It was time. It was time to finally start living. I left the house that day feeling and looking like myself and have never gone back.

Since that cool November day, my life has been knocked from side to side. There have been some mountain top joys and some deep and lonely sorrow. My body has changed as my breasts have developed and fat has redistributed. The incredible feeling of euphoria I felt the first time I put a shirt on without a bra and had a noticeable chest is indescribable. I rarely ever get misgendered any more, and when I do, I'm able to kindly correct people and move on. My relationship with my younger sister has blossomed into something so beautiful, and I've made friendships that are closer than ever. Every time I leave the house now, I'm excited for what the day has in store for me. I finally feel comfortable in my own skin. Not just comfortable, euphoric. It's a feeling that took me 33 years to find.

But the highs were not without the lows. My relationship with my mom was tense for a while. She felt like she was taken off guard by the change and wished to be included more in my process. My relationship with my brother had suffered, which I talk a little bit about in a poem called "The Brother He Lost," found later in this chapter. And my relationship with my partner, Kendra, shifted from a romantic partnership to that of close friendship, our 9 years of marriage soon to end in divorce. In the last year and a half, I've discovered more about myself, my sexuality, the things that bring me joy, and the things that steal my peace than I had in the 33 years prior.

The potential to start new romantic partnerships and to explore my sexuality free from the constraints of Christendom and cultural norms is very exciting. This could be an over share for some of you, but you made it this far… from personal experience, I can say a testosterone fueled orgasm is nothing compared to one fueled by estrogen. It's like comparing what it's like to ride a wave in a wave pool to riding a wave in the ocean. They're longer, deeper, scarier, and so much more of a rush. Even the simple experience of being turned on is a completely different experience. The first time I kissed a boy left me swooning, like I literally almost collapsed.

The future beyond is bound to be full of so much more growth and change. I'm grateful to be living in an era and place in the world where these changes are accepted. I'm excited to continue living my truth and finding out who I am. I'm excited to make and nurture these friendships that have started blossoming. I'm excited for my body to continue developing and becoming the woman she was always meant to be.

So, dear reader, in the poems that follow, I hope you're able to see the fears, the joys, and the excitement I try to convey. I hope you're able to feel the deep pain of self-discovery and the incredible growth that comes with it. I hope you're able to continue forward on your own path with the same excitement and abandon that I am.

All My Love,

Aubrey

What I Wanted

I wish I had received it,
Unconditional from the start
Known I deserved it,
The way I knew in my heart,

I always fell short
of the standards for perfection,
and couldn't make myself worthy
of any love and affection,

Your 'unconditional love'
was given with condition,
So I kept trying to earn it
with mounting desperation,
I longed, so deeply,
for that intimate connection.

One not understood
by words nor by phrases,
nor truly experienced
by hugs and by praises.

For the love that's passed on

from parent to child

Not romantic, nor spiritual,

something fierce yet mild.

I never received

that needed gift,

So I struggle to pass it on,

to find the strength to lift,

This web of 'if…

then I'll love you fully,'

As fake as a drawer

of plastic costume jewelry.

Tides and Storms

At rest my mind races

with selfish thoughts

Some are realized

others are lost.

Is this all just a game?

A self-deception?

Or of desperation

for lost connection?

But…

How could I lose something I never had?

Something I merely glimpsed, like a passing fad.

You see…

I'd only been seen through the eyes of another

as the gifted son or exampled brother.

But as the clock still moves
My lenses fade.
From son to daughter
a change is made.

So…

I chose myself to truly love

to haven't another below nor above.
But with lens lost, I struggled to see
To know by what image
To create what is me.

So line
by tedious line
I write
and I think
I begin casting off
and I pray not to sink.

Though these seas are restless

and these tides are high

I'm more willing to feel,

more willing to cry

more willing to love all that's inside.

To know my body

to love her

before she dies.

So as storms gather power, and winds fills my sails

this connection with myself is all that prevails.

For it's not some great treasure

lost out at sea.

She is patiently waiting

somewhere

within me....

A Brother Lost

He lost a brother,

his companion,

Where he found himself in another.

He lost a brother,

his confidant,

His teammate when he hadn't another.

He lost a brother,

his sparring partner,

Who'd continue the banter ever further.

The one who was with him through divorce,

through break-ups, through scars.

Scars they bore together,

in a room at the top of the stairs.

He lost a brother,

but not by death, nor fighting, nor chance.

He lost his brother

because his brother discovered her dance.

She stepped with a new and revitalized soul.

She was no longer broken; she'd become something whole.

She started gliding through life as a faraway stranger,

one that knew him so intimately, yet there was a disclaimer.

She would never again be the brother he knew,

who'd stand by his side when he said his, "I do's"

in the way he did for her when her love was true.

It was scary to consider that who she'd become

was someone he couldn't connect to, was too different from.

This brother he knew through decades of life,

who'd been there for him through joys and through strife.

He felt she'd betray him,

like others had done.

Like she'd use it against him,

this knowledge she'd won.

He wanted his friend back,

the one that he lost.

He wanted his brother back,

but at what scary cost?

She wanted that too but struggled to speak it.
She'd lost a brother too, though somewhere beneath it,
was a brand new relationship, one she wanted unwrapped,
a brand new connection, just longing to be tapped.

So with tears in her eyes, she said in a whisper,
"I'm sorry you lost your brother,
but please, I beg you, find me as your sister."

Reflection of Dreams

It's never easy to find the words to say
that fully captures how my feelings lay.
To be witnessed at my truest depth
To be seen, fully, intimately, left without breath.

I never thought they'd actually see
All I've seen myself to be
That I'd never live in such a time
that I am yours and you are mine.

Tangible perfection in the love we create.
A beautiful shift in the fabric of space.

Time simply stops.
No ticking, no clock.

Hands clinging to tender palms
Discover peace, discover calm.
But the world is still begging for our attention
using its chaos to break our intimate affection.

So returning again to the brevity of time

We let go of the moment and slip from our rhyme.

A sad return to that old rhythm: "life"

Waiting in the tension, in need of a knife.

I seek for relief in the strength of your embrace

to succumb to the bliss, to succumb to the chase.

To once again be fully me, fully seen.

As my reality becomes merely, a reflection of dreams.

Please Complete Me

Consumed by his confidence

Quickly, "I" becoming "us"

A reckless pursuit and loss of self

Endless charm blocking the hurt I felt.

My recently broken heart, I wore

Low on my sleeve, attracting his lure

But my shattered heart reflected his own

Wounds still unhealed left us together, alone.

But the pain still came with opportunity

To define more clearly my need for boundaries

to not lose myself in the arms of a lover

that there was so much of me left to discover.

Another cannot define who I am,

Identity can't be found in a person or program

There's no way to restrain the boundless infinity,

of a love both given and received by me.

Thirst & Love

There's that moment
when you meet someone new.
That moment of attempted connection
of roots reaching for water
deciding if it will be worth the stretch

That reaching has left me dry
over and over -
finding nothing but sand
barren land
in someone willing to make space
but unwilling to sustain

just an empty well
long since drained

& Dust

Is it naivety or desperation

that keeps me exploring this desert?

searching for connection

for completion

for love

for affection

Hoping someday

I'd find someone

with water to give

before my well

holds nothing but dust

to offer in return.

The One

Believing he
Completed me
With covered eyes
I couldn't see
The only one for me
was me.

To All of Life's Questions

A single spark,

a flash of light

a long-darkened void drifts out of sight.

A single touch

my soul expands

my heart finds rest in the palm of my hands.

Discovering answers

a taste of the mystery

The one great minds ponder through history.

Of hope,

of light,

of growth,

of love

From the firing of a neuron,

to the wings of a dove.

The one great mystery of life itself

Unanswered by the books on all the shelves.

Still, onward I search,

In words and in dreams

For purpose, for pleasure,

to love to extremes.

No answer I find

in this hopeless pursuit

Simply more questions

More dark caves to loot.

Life without love

can't be lived to its fullest

Only for myself, can love be at its truest.

The potential exists though,

for sorrow, for pain

But without the capacity for loss

there's no gain.

So the questions persist

without answers to speak of

So I succumb to the mystery

and instead choose

to be love.

To Love Myself Again

There is a restless weight burdening my soul,

Stealing my satisfaction, hiding me from the whole.

Relaxing my mind, it twists to fractals

Like a moss-covered rock that begins to roll.

My past drags me away from the present, the light

I find love divided, but I choose to fight.

Fighting to recover all that time stole.

I'm learning to love with all of my might.

I long for connection, one I once held close.

An intimate relationship, a long dormant rose.

One that needs to be tended and moved to the light.

A love I once nurtured but has long since plateaued.

A love for myself is what needs to be found.

A passion for me, hidden deep underground.

It took work to bury, right under my nose.

But it's not lost forever, for I can hear it resound.

Till it's all been dug up, the work is not done

While it desperately yearns for its time in the sun

So I'll continue the work, till love is unbound

to pass on the gift of self-love to my sons.

Aubrey Jane Jones

inward

Dear Small Voice... 87

Values... 90

Slaves Without a Master............................. 92

To Be Seen.. 94

Losses & Gains.. 96

Estrogen... 104

Introduction: *Inward*

Dear Reader,

On April 20, 2022, my name was officially changed from what it was to Aubrey Jane Jones. Kendra, my kids, and my mom all joined me at the courthouse that day for my assigned time slot when I would stand before the judge and plead my case, in hopes they would tap their gavel and approve my motion.

The day was not without its roadblocks. When I sat down, I was handed a document by the judge listing outstanding judgements filed under my previous name that totaled over $200,000. They wanted to make sure I wasn't changing my name to escape any of those, so I was peppered with questions about work I had done and places I had lived before we even got to my proposed case.

This case of mistaken identity was a lot to pile on top of everything that was going on in my head that day. On top of having to prove to this judge that I am, in fact, a transwoman, this accusation added layers and layers of fear onto my anxiety, already thick with trepidation. I felt the eyes of the judge piercing me as I denied all of the claims he was making, looking for any reason to not grant me my appeal. My chest tightened. Would this be the end? Would it all be over before it even started? These questions were screaming in my head as I tried to calmly answer his queries.

Once I satisfied the court that I was not the person they were looking for, they got to the matter at hand. There were three things on the docket: my name change order, a motion to waive the publication requirement, and a motion to seal the record.

During the name change motion, the judge asked me why I wanted to change my name. I had to explain to the court-room that I was a trans woman and wanted a name that better reflected my gender. After the judge creepily eyed me up and down a few times, my name change was approved.

Next was the motion to waive the publication requirement for the name change, a rule which requires people to publish their old name, their current address, and their new name in two local newspapers for two weeks. You can probably see why this would be a dangerous thing to do for someone in my position.

He asked me why I wanted to waive the requirement, to which I responded that I feared for my and my family's safety if my status as a trans person was advertised in the paper. His response still astounds me. He said, "Are you *actually* afraid for your safety?" My jaw dropped. I quoted a couple figures to him that I had prepared ahead of time that mentioned the physical harassment and homicide committed against transwomen in the last year. After a scoff from the judge, my request was granted.

There's so much meaning in a name, so much of a person's identity is tied to the string of syllables they use to identify themselves to the world. I was so happy walking out of the courthouse that I cried. I cried all the way to the DMV, then cried some more when I walked out with my new license, complete with a new picture, and gender marker. Something shifted in me that day. The new reality I was creating was recognized by the culture I was a part of. It felt amazing.

My identity as a woman, as a transperson, as Aubrey, is so important to me. For decades, my identity was something I wanted to hide from. Never feeling connected to it, I minimized it. But now, I'm so proud of who I am, who I'm becoming, and for the life I get to live now.

In this chapter, I turn inward. I turn to the things that were, and still are happening beneath the surface. I hope you get a chance to see deeper into who I am. I hope you can be inspired and look inward as well, to discover more fully who you are, your identity, and that you are the only person that can truly love you.

All My Love,

Aubrey

Dear Small Voice

Thank you

Thank you for protecting me

Thank you for strengthening me

Thank you for pushing me

for guiding me

for being patient with me

for grieving with me

for loving me.

Thank you for celebrating the good

and for mourning the loss

for giving all that you could

for all the love you came across.

You gave me all that you could give

nourishment, grace, an appetite to live.

You gave me truth and authenticity,

which I ignored in lieu of simplicity.

I'm sorry for the years I didn't listen,

for vilifying your love and your wisdom.

I regret not trusting your truth and your promise

For not loving you completely as my inner goddess.

Held back by fear, by self-rejection

unwilling to accept the body I lived in.

I treated her like she was worthless, a waste.

I rejected her fully, forgotten, erased.

And we did a good job of keeping her buried

I weighed you down with my burdens,

which you willingly carried.

Now that they're lifted, she's starting to rise.

Boundless and free, she'll take to the skies.

So please, I beg you, be patient with me.

Learning to trust you and hoping desperately,

that all the damage and scars I still wear,

won't keep her from feeling

all the love that's still there.

All My Love,

Aubrey

Values

Honesty, boldness, and reconciliation
Pride in authenticity and deep conversation
Nature, motherhood, love, and embrace
Comfort and clarity, escaping the rat-race.

Hope and renewal, pain born of growth
Family and friends and the ones I love most
Respect, sincerity, taking part in creation
Fresh eyes, new ideas, and relaxing vacations.

Naps and cuddles, towels straight from the dryer
Getting lost, getting found, soft music around a camp-fire
Peaceful nights, and starry skies
The feeling of surrender after a much-needed cry.

These are the things that drive me on,
To wake up every day to greet the new dawn,
To look up to the sky and welcome the start,
Each day, every moment, as a masterful work of art.

So when fear and when loneliness draw my well dry,

When life wraps me up in a tangle of lies,

When there's nothing to pull me up out of that hole,

I turn inward to be lifted on the wings of my soul.

Slaves Without a Master

My sorrow thickens,
as does the armor I force myself to carry.
The weight of it,
comparable only to the loss.

The loss of self,
of walls,
of love,
of hope,
of plans,
of future.

Where is my refuge?
From where can I find my strength?

Not from those that call out, "Lord, Lord,"
yet set so unattainable a standard.

Not from those that say, "Love Wins!"
yet call my identity a slander.

From where, then, can I find my hope?
To whom do I turn to rediscover my answer?

For God does not exist,
but in the hearts of slaves without a master

Some say, "Search within yourself
to find your peace, to find your pasture."

And maybe within,
there's some space to forgive,

So I searched and I searched,
And all I found inside
was a sad little girl
who never got a chance
to thrive.

To Be Seen

To truly be seen, for all that I am
To be known and be loved, all over again
To find rest, to find peace
To find hope and release

Free from the pressure to be all I am not
Free from the expectation to live my cast lot

To be witnessed as my open, transparent self
To be understood, so my heart may be held
To be me, truly me, in all of my wholeness
To be loved to my depth and accepted in boldness

From the top of my head
to the tips of my toes
From the core of my heart
to the breadth of my soul

This grouping of atoms, my soul now indwells
Is temporary and broken, every organ, every cell

But with soul laid bare, naked, and afraid

Wounds left visible by the choices I've made

She seeks hope in acceptance, in love freely given

She seeks peace in the tapestry of life that she's woven

For life is not perfect, so to be seen in her flaws

to be seen in her fullness, behind all her walls

Is the greatest gift she could ever hope to give

A gift to herself, a chance for a life fully lived

So if such a gift is ever offered to you

Please handle with care, her valuable truth

For nothing hurts more than a soul left rejected

So receive it with tenderness and compassionately accept it

Keep it close to your heart,

protect it from shame

Because one day, quite soon,

you may need the same.

Losses & Gains

I.

I get lost in my head
when I think of what's past
What's been lost, what's been gained
as time moves too fast.

After thirty-three years,
twelve weeks, and three days,
My real life began
As I filled in all the grays.

The moment things changed
turned my world upside down
A fuller joy, a deeper love,
at last, could be found.

With a flash of excitement,
my heart clearly knew
So I leapt into the unknown
and I actually flew.

II.

I flew as high and as fast as I could,

I was free

To live as the woman

I was meant to be.

But with new light and perspective,

soon I would find

There'd be no way to go back,

no way to rewind

No way to recover

The ones left behind.

Family and friends,

all those I loved,

were stricken with grief

where there once had been love.

They considered my truth
as a loss of what'd been
Mourning our memories
before her sprang from him.

I felt the loss too,
but from somewhere quite different.
I felt sorrow after losing
The bonds I felt loved in.

The love of my life
for eleven long years
ended our marriage
me drowning in tears.

We tried to maintain it,
but the spark flickered out.
Like a light switch was flicked
from being on to off.

Friendships maintained

through decades, some more

Now solely existed

in stories and lore.

The love that was there

between friends disappeared.

Confirming the loss

I had anxiously feared.

III.

But with losses came gains,
and with every new dawn
Love found me again.
New relationships formed.

New friendships, new ideas,
new joys, new connections
That didn't compare me
to the person I'd once been.

Ones that loved me for me
in this body I lived in.

When my masculine lines,
hard set, began softening
escaping reality
became far less compelling.

I'd lived all my life

in this body feeling broken

Now she was becoming

a place I felt whole in.

IV.

But a sadness took shape
that is tough to explain.
My family felt sorrow
toward what I felt as gain.

My body was changing,
I found joy in my truth
But instead of sharing my delight,
they held a pain I couldn't soothe.

Revealing my excitement
only brought pain
Bittersweet celebration
like a cold summer rain.

Rain coming with haste
with not a cloud in the sky
Plans changed, hope waned
as the world starts to cry.

But my truth is now shown

for the whole world to see

An incredible gift

from me to me.

Aubrey Jane Jones

Estrogen

A deeper connection to my emotions
A bluer sky, a grander ocean
A heart that's free to a greater experience
to discover and grow, be grateful and curious.

My body becoming who I knew her to be
to look in the mirror, to forever be me.
My face, my hair, my skin, my breasts
My soul now embracing all the effects.

What I knew in my heart, I now see in pictures
This beautiful woman, and I get to be her
Who, my whole life, I longed to meet.
This person I've prayed and hoped for desperately.

This mother I've become can more deeply love
My children, my partner, and those I've made friends of.
This tiny green pill has made this change so genuine
My life, my experience, my body on estrogen.

outward

Winter's Death 113

Happily Ever After 115

Motherhood 117

Sprinkle 119

Dear Kendra 121

Introduction: *Outward*

Dear Reader,

This last section consists of a few poems that I've written for and about the people in my life that I dearly love. All these people hold a special place in my heart and these few words don't do any justice to the profound impact they've had on me.

I originally wrote "Winter's Death" as a reflection on the winter solstice, personifying the sun as the woman in the poem. But the more I read it, the more my own words were speaking to me regarding death as it pertains to the people we love, our elders. It was one of the first poems I was able to share with my grandmother, and I realized right then that I wrote it for her. She has a beautiful and loving soul and has been a powerful example of womanhood in my life. I have so much love for her.

"Happily Ever After" probably sticks out the most in this collection because it doesn't necessarily pertain to anyone in particular. When I wrote it, I was thinking of all the little girls that grew up watching the same 90's Disney movies that I did, receiving the same screwed up messages about love and happiness. The biggest internal shift I needed to make after getting out into the dating world again was to stop looking for someone to complete me. I needed to stop looking for validation from someone else and start turning inward instead. I hoped to reframe the idea of happily ever after, not by saying it can't exist, but by saying the source can only come from within.

I wrote "Motherhood" for my mom and all the moms that give so much of themselves to their children, whether biological, adopted, or gained through connection. I'm so thankful for all the mothers that have shaped me into the mother I am to my kids today.

Early in 2023, a close friend of mine shared the news that he and his partner were pregnant! I was filled with joy for them in such a profound way, partly because bringing life into the world is amazing, but also because of the tragedy they'd experienced in their past. In the time I've known them, they've lost twins, not once, but twice. Both times were in the later stages of pregnancy. Mitch told me all about this new joy that he was feeling and when they went to get their recent checkup, the doctor confirmed that there was only one fetus. I asked if they had a name picked out to call their new baby while it was still in utero, he said they were calling them Sprinkle, because they were currently the size of a sprinkle. I wrote "Sprinkle" for them.

"Dear Kendra" was written for my ex-wife, Kendra. She has been monumental in my growth as a person and as a woman. I know, no matter what the future holds, she will always have a place in my heart.

I'm sure many of you have been touched by a grandmother, a lover, a mother, and a friend in the ways I have. For those that are hurting, I hope you can find refuge within yourself, that you can find the love that exists deep within your soul. I know it's so much easier said than done, but I promise it's there. In the meantime, please know how much I love you, how much I care for you. Even though I may never meet you or know your name, I love you. Your light is worth shining, is worth bringing to the world. It wouldn't be the same without you.

All My Love,

Aubrey

Winter's Death

Day breaks
and the dawn strides
as She takes one last ride
across the skies
on this long and cold night
She drifts off to die

She dies, fully conscious and feeling,
finding rest in non-existence,
She extinguishes Her gleaming
beyond the horizon,
finding death and release
Her light burns out
total and complete

darkness descends, like an enemy it seems,
cutting off Her children, who drift off to dreams
they long for the light
for the warmth that She brings.

but out of the dark arises a call

to all of the living

both the big and the small

"have hope," She exclaims

in a long desperate sigh

"after this death

will soon come My rise"

then, from out of the darkness

She's birthed all anew

all the ground thick with cold morning dew

Her children awaken

knowing Her promise was true

because the night never lasts

no matter how dark

for Morning and newness

need naught but a Spark

For Viola

Happily Ever After

The desire to live happily ever after
For a life filled with joy and smiles and laughter
A hoped-for reality in a princess's promise
To unveil a prince that's both strong and honest

To ever be satisfied in another's arms
The purest of loves from her dear prince of charms
To discover completeness in tenderness and care
As soft loving fingers glide through her hair.

But this promise can't be real, it's merely a deceit
A lofty expectation he could never hope to meet.
The deepest of love needs not wait for another
From not a prince, nor a friend, nor a sister, nor mother

The greatest of loves she could ever hope to find
Comes not with age, nor planning, nor place, nor time,
But from somewhere inside her very own heart,
A love never removed, nor torn into parts.

This happily ever after she's so desperate for
Pours out from within the depth of her core
Needing only to look, she'll soon discover
She's the only one that truly can love her.

Motherhood

Gentleness, compassion, empathy, and love.

The ferocity of a tiger, with the grace of a dove.

Hands overflowing with tenderness and with care.

Prepared to defend against any who'd dare

A lover, a healer, a tutor, a partner.

A shoulder to cry on, a generous listener.

A defender of secrets and teller of hard truths,

Told in a way that you know they love you.

A keeper of promises, a foundation to build on.

And willing to sacrifice, even die for their children.

An encourager, a giver of endless affection.

Their motivation not thanks, nor want for attention.

Mothers don't come from birth, they are made.

Created by the love that they endlessly gave.

A spirit that's both tenacious and tender.

That comes not by birth, nor by blood, nor by gender.

I give thanks to all mothers, especially mine.

To the one I was born to, and ones gained over time.

The example of motherhood they forged in me,

Will forever be etched in who my children will be.

Sprinkle

To lose not one but two, not once but twice,

familiar sorrow claims their joy, claims its price.

Four hearts entwined with a father's and mother's,

Who lie in shared tears, under soaked sheets and covers.

Their incarnation of love, of dreams, of hope,

became a tragedy, a loss, an endless struggle to cope.

Their dreams nearly realized, mere moments away,

now empty existence, day and night, night and day.

But the hope of a parent, or so that it seems,

turns desperation into prayer, and prayers into dreams.

Dreams of a future, of eager expectation,

push them to leap, to take part in creation.

Boldly, courageously, they cast anxiety aside.

Again, two becoming one, a husband and bride.

Then, only together, on trembling feet,

one hand grasps the other and ears hear a beat.

This inexpressible joy, a gift from above,

what was longed for, begotten. A small sprinkle of love.

What power? What hope; did come from this sound?

Just proof that their love is a love without bounds.

For Mitch & Tanya - May the love you share continue to inspire others as it has inspired me.

Dear Kendra

Dear Kendra, my thanks for your endless support,
knowing now our bright future will end in divorce.
The fire once burning so brightly between us.
Is but smoke and ash that smolders beneath us.

I hope that one day we may each use the last spark
as a catalyst to bring about an incredible start.
When we take our steps forward, both growing and learning,
Remembering our paths are not ending, they're beginning.

I will always be grateful for all the love and the care,
for your support and the promise you'd always be there.
Thank you for all the years we've spent together
/I want you to know how much you've made my life better.

I'll always be there for you; however you need me.
It's the least I can do with how truly you loved me.
And if you need space, I promise I'll give you that.
But I certainly hope that's not where we arrive at.

So no matter where tides take us from here,

whether the going is rough or the weather is clear

I need you to promise, for our boys, you'll be strong,

that they'll always have a place where they're loved and belong.

And whatever happens, please, don't take them away.

They're the light of my life and at the end of the day,

there's nothing I wouldn't do to be sure they're okay.

I'll love them, and love you, till my last breath fades away.

All My Love,

Aubrey

Aubrey Jane Jones

Dear Reader,

Here's a sentence that I never thought I would ever say: thank you for taking the time to read my book. I hope that you have been able to resonate with some of the stories and +themes that I wrote about. At the coffee shop where I work, my goal is that every customer can leave feeling better than when they arrived. I hope the same is true for you after reading my poems.

Before the last page, there are some people in that I need to give a HUGE thank you to:

To my sister Morgan, thank you for believing in me, listening to my poems, and encouraging me to listen to my inner voice. Thank you for supporting me fully, from day one. You have inspired me to be the powerful woman I am today.

To Becki, thank you for loving me through it all. Thank you for being there for me at my darkest time and brightest times. Not least of all, thank you for encouraging me to start playing roller derby.

To all the girls in Rockstar Roller Derby, you have brought more love into my life than I ever expected possible. You welcomed me into your sisterhood with so much care and made me feel more than welcome. I would never have been able to make it through the last year without you.

To my therapist Armando, thank you for seeing me though and for believing in me, for being the first person to hear one of my poems and inspiring me to keep writing.

To my parents: Carol and Gary, thank you for believing in me, for believing in my dreams, for telling me that I could be anything I wanted to be. I know you didn't expect this to be the result but thank you for loving me anyway.

To Kendra, thank you for supporting me through it all. Thank you for listening to me and believing me when I shared my truth with you. Thank you for fiercely loving me though nine and a half years of marriage, two kids, and my transition. Thank you for always telling me to live authentically. Thank you for letting me borrow your clothes, for lending me your make-up, and for telling me I'm beautiful. Thank you for not killing me while I went through the emotional roller coaster of a second puberty. Thank you for loving our kids so well.

And finally, thank you to all the people that listened to me read my poems, I would never have published this if not for so many of you telling me I should.

Lastly, dear reader, thank you for purchasing and reading my work. I poured my entire self into these pages, and I hope you were able to find just as much healing reading them as I found writing them.

All My Love,

Aubrey

ABOUT THE *Author*

Aubrey is a mother of two, aspiring coffee master, certified spiritual coach, and now, an author. She started writing *All My Love, Aubrey* in November of 2022, exactly one year after taking her first lifesaving dose of hormone replacement therapy, writing her first poem, "Slaves without a Master," on the last page of a journal she kept while working in ministry after a particularly emotional therapy session. After getting that small part of her story out on paper, she discovered, for the first time in her life, how much healing can come from writing.

Prior to starting her transition in 2021, Aubrey worked as a full-time youth pastor for 11 years after attending Eastern University to study youth ministry. She left the church and organized religion at the end of 2020 during a global pandemic, 21 years after "giving her life to Christ." Many of the poems you find in this book are the result of her processing the trauma she experienced with the church and the lasting impact it's had on her.

Aubrey hopes that her readers transgender and cisgender alike, can see themselves in the poems she's penned. More than anything, she wishes that her experience in leaving Christianity and living her truth will give hope to people in the LGBTQIA+ community. That they know that they are not alone.

When Aubrey is not momming or tasting coffees with her coworkers, she spends her time writing, playing with her dog Roscoe, foraging for wild mushrooms, and skating for the Rockstar Roller Derby team out of Pottstown, PA who have been an incredible source of love and support over the last year.

To connect with Aubrey, you're invited to email her at aubreyjones.poetry@gmail.com. She would love to hear from you.

www.ingramcontent.com/pod-product-compliance
Lightning Source LLC
Chambersburg PA
CBHW070907160726
48004CB00003B/1268